Our Paths In Life
POEMS

Our Paths In Life
POEMS

KR HARBERT

REDHAWK
PUBLICATIONS

Our Paths in Life

Copyright © 2023 Ken Harbert

All rights reserved. This book or parts thereof may not be reproduced in any form, stored in any retrieval system, or transmitted in any form by any means—electronic, mechanical, photocopy, recording, or otherwise—without prior written permission of the publisher, except as provided by United States of America copyright law. For permission requests, write to the publisher, at "Attention: Permissions Coordinator," at the address below.

Redhawk Publications
The Catawba Valley Community College Press
2550 US Hwy 70 SE
Hickory NC 28602
https://redhawkpublications.com

ISBN: 978-1-959346-10-4

Library of Congress Number: 2023935917

Printed in the United States of America

Cover Photograph: Ken Harbert
Cover Design & Layout: Michelle Benoit
Edited by Patrick Bizzaro

redhawkpublications.com

DEDICATION

First, to Aylen and Ian our future. Second, to all those on the paths that have been within my universe. My universe encompasses family both given and chosen. To my given family you are my forever. To my chosen family of friends: you have made our world better by being dedicated to service above self. I offer my observations in the poems that follow to all those women and men who are first responders, nurses, physicians, physician associates, combat corpsmen and medics, and others that walk that path that offers us a much better and safer world. May we all live in peace, finding laugher within ourselves, hope in our futures and understanding with each other.

PREFACE

This book is about the paths we all have in life, and it is based on my observations from my many years in helping others help themselves which in turn helped me better understand my own path in life.

It is about people we know: our families, both given and chosen, along with workers, lovers, patients, friends, and veterans. Each of them gives assistance to others on their life journeys and on their life paths. We never know where our paths or crossroads will lead us each day. Yet we wake up and take that first step forward every day after day. We travel life's paths, frequently encountering crossroads, some different while often the same. We rarely know what to expect, which is also what makes life worth living.

We travel over roads of marriage, divorce, love, hate, illnesses, pain, suffering, worry, joy, trauma, care and sometimes compassion. We never know if a chosen path will be good or bad. Sometimes going down a path offers a thrill and adventure. Other times it is a moment of time in life best forgotten. Our life's paths are simply our unwritten poems, which is why I've chosen to make my observations in the poems that make up this volume.

All of us travel down these paths and stop at their crossroads. May we all be safe, thankful for the good and remain ever cautious of the bad. Yet it takes everyone in our lives to offer directions to find that right path during our journeys.

So, please join along on *Our Paths in Life*, written in hopes that the words may help all of us understand the crossroads and appreciate the right path.

TABLE OF CONTENTS

Part One: Thoughts Along the Paths of Life   1

Paths 3
First Steps 5
Passion 7
Shadow Walks 9
Time 11
String Theory 12
Fear 13
Mistakes 14
The Eyes Have It 15
All Too Often 16
The Quantum Roadway 17
The Journal 18
Mind Clouds 19
Vision 21
Life 22
Life Is Like Sailing 23
The Older I Get 25
If 27
One Or Fifty, Which Way to Go 28
Life And Death 31
Sometimes 32
Shifts In Time 33
Age 34
Sometimes Life 35
Life, Love, And The Meditation Stone 36
Need 38
Changing 39
Silence 41
The Movie Of Our Lives 42
Music Abides 43
Ear Worms 44

Part Two: Places Along These Paths   47

Defining Life and Love Within A Sushi Bar . . . 49
The Tao Road To Taos. 50
Star Dust. 52
A Long Table Of Others 55
Sunsets. 56
Don't Really Know .57
Wichita City Blues. 58
Days And Days. 59
Home 60
Swarthmore In Fall 62
The Hem/Onc Trip 64
Lost Again In LA. .66
The Night the Music Fell from The Skies. . . .67
Journeys 68
Nijmegen 69
Same Stars, Same Night. 70
Cinco De Mio 71

Part Three: People We Meet on Our Paths, Guiding Us, Showing Us The Way, Helping Us Through The Curves   73

Green Chili Cheeseburgers 75
Rainbow Dancer .77
Music Daydreams 79
My Physics Daughter 81
M 82
Words Never Written 84
My Puzzle Queen. 86
A Good Mother 88
Enablers 89
Always 91
The Paddle 92
I Have Been Lucky. 93

Dave And the Golden Bridges 94
Catch And Release. 96
Goodbye. 98
So Much Alike 99
Also 100
Bedtime. 101
My Brother, The Mensch 102
Jerry, The Seadog 104
He Keeps On Trying 105
Friends Or Lovers 106
Connections 107
Barb, My True Earth Mother 108
Weird 109
The Muse. 110
To A Long-Lost Son 111
My Favorite Cookie 113
Spirit Rider. 114
Old Friends. 116
Epitaph. 117
Face Fix 118
Your Sense Of Meaning 119

Part Four: Those Who Provide Service Above Themselves 121

Veterans 123
Survivor 125
Going Back. 127
Will You Remember My Name 129
An Eighty-Year-Old Man 130
Memorial Day 133
When Darkness Looms 135
Van, Again 136
Brothers And Sisters In Granite 139
Life Savers Then.... Caregivers Forever 141
My Return 143

So It Began. 144
God Loves the Grunts 146
Wall Of Names. 148
Walking Dead 151

Part Five: Those That Care For Others 153

PA's We Are 155
His Last Breath 157
Ruth, The Change Agent 159
Bypass Next Day. 160
Patient Advocates 161
And Then There Were Angels. 163
Why Do You Do What You Do. 164
Life Meets Death. 166
The Art Of Medicine 168
I Cared 169
EMT, RN, PA, PhD She Is. 171

PART ONE:
THOUGHTS ALONG THE PATHS OF LIFE

PATHS

We always choose the paths of our lives
We try
We fail
We wish for better
We then try again
Yet there they are
In front of us day by day
Always there
Seducing us with visions
Wishes that swim like millions of tiny fishes
Finding the right path is never easy
It just is what it is
Hope for tomorrow

FIRST STEPS

Our paths of life are never
Made alone

We follow the footsteps of so many
They guide us
They love us
They mentor us
They pray for us

So is it any wonder
That some of us are lucky to go together
In chosen and given families

With a mom
A dad
A son
A sister
A daughter
A friend
A lover
A partner
All our family

Knowing all in life begins
Together
With that first step

PASSION

Is it in our hearts
Is it in our work
Do we grow it ourselves
Do we learn it from others
Do we just know it as it occurs
Do we find it makes us at peace with ourselves
Or are we driven to find something more
Passion and peace no more no less

SHADOW WALKS

You can never walk away
From your shadow
It follows you forever

Being, seeing, needing more time
Unlike peter pan
You cannot just tack it up
Or wear it when you wish

It's there beside and behind you
Full of what was, what is,
Lost hopes, lost loves, lost dreams
As you do that infamous
Shadow walks

TIME

Time equals the minute by minute
Kodak moments of our lives
Days and weeks go by
Months and years race by

Yet the younger we are
Time seems to slowly add up

The older we get
Somehow it is like sand between our fingers
The tighter we hold onto it
The more we seem to lose it
And the more precious
We believe it is to us

We find it gone
Time moves on
Yet it seems like only yesterday

STRING THEORY

String theory is life coming together thread by thread or is it
Are we part of a constant string of moving space called time
Do we drift between the now and then and the maybe
Were we once there
In a different way
Maybe a different gender
A different person
Does that forgotten sense of being there
Our touch,
Our comfort,
Our knowledge,
Our history,
Or does it follow us forever through the dimensions
For are we simply in an ever-circling string of time
Free drifting back and forth
Among the endless seas of space and time

FEAR

Worry
Anxiety
Unrelating
Unknown
Unsettled
Unwanted
Life

MISTAKES

The problems with caring for people
Are the mistakes you might make

Those that affect their lives, their families, their futures
No matter where you go
What you do

You always know
When and how you will own your mistakes
Whether you know it or not

THE EYES HAVE IT

Brilliant yet muddy green orbits
that changed color when the anger rose
as if their jaded context were emerging
from a distant, yet fiery, deep green forest

A true contradiction
Making her many admirers
and her adversaries to underestimate who she is

She cares nothing about the perspectives of others
Wanting only those in her close circle of friends and family

She passes the show leaving a scent of liquid vanilla
Making all aware of it as a perfect moment

Hiding, yet revealing at times, the depth of injury
Deep down in her soul, trauma from long ago
Hidden but as cold as stone
Soulful bruises never ever seen
Chiseled there by the ancient's troubles

She always leaves you
with the feeling that she always had more to say
But try as she could
Words never came out for better or worse
The eyes have it forever changing who she is or will be
now and forever

ALL TOO OFTEN

All too often
We forget
To accept
That sometimes
We meet
We work
We trust
We love
We believe

In someone
Yet sometimes
We meet
We work with
We Trust
We love
We believe,
In silly stupid hurtful people

So goes our karma
Seeking out the good
Seeking out the real from the not real

Occasionally having the good and common sense
To know the difference
It's this special sense
That all to often
Guides our paths in life

THE QUANTUM ROADWAY

Do we all experience past lives
If so, is there a quantum thread roadway
That connects us to it all

Do we all have a deep subtle thread
That connects the past to present to future

Shadowing us in a way
Revealed maybe only once or twice in our present timeline
Do we all have that sense of deja vu

Knowing that we have been there or here before
Are we just a seamless thread of the absolute
Past, present, future flowing into the whirlpool of eternity
Can we sense it or is there a deeper guilt or absolution of time and space
Stardust moving on forever

THE JOURNAL

I open it carefully
Removing the old leather ties
Casual yet direct
careful slow movements
Then comes the closure
Is it too early
Or is it too late

After the words have left my mind
Traveling to my hand
Then to the pen
Absorbed by the paper
Firmly there in black and white

It's a Zen moment made in closing
Swiftly, forcefully tying the leather around itself
Keeping those thoughts to myself
Hoping as I close the book, I close my mind
Closure for all else with the simple process
Of that leather strap on leather
Mind over body
Deed over thought
So the mind tells the body
You are finished
For now

MIND CLOUDS

Sometimes it's hard to touch your dreams
We always search for the Jungian meanings
Thinking they offer more than we understand
Sometimes we never know our dreams
Sometimes they haunt us with what we never wish to have
Sometimes they scare us because they seem to know more
Sometimes we learn more than we wanted to
Sometimes we just say "aha that's the meaning there"
Sometimes we touch the mind clouds, and they help us move on

VISION

Photographers have light
Sailors have wind
Writers have words
Believers have prayers
We all have our own visions
But can we really see
What's there

Right now in front of us

LIFE

Life is just what it is
Never perfect
Sometimes excellent
Rarely wonderful
Never more
Never less
It's all up to us
To accept it
For what it is
Just living for the now
Better or worse
It is what it is

LIFE IS LIKE SAILING

You face endless waves of time moving onward

Facing uncertain currents that push and pull your soul

Rising and falling tides of joy and sorrow

New and interesting harbors of life

So, start with a good sail plan

Get wind in your sails, when in doubt breath out

Always know where your north is

Understand where the important points of sail are in your life past and present

Stay on a steady track and be consistent in your course, follow the plan

Involve a team of levelheaded crew that believe in you and your lifelong ever-changing plan

Understand the hazards and rewards that lie ahead and those that are behind you

Always know your limits as a captain and in your life

THE OLDER I GET

The older I get
The more I appreciate

Those things ignored far too long in life
Friends, soul mates, family

The sound and feel of the ocean
The bright azure sky full of endless clouds
The birthing of each day with a new beginning
A sunset full of multi colors

The smell and laughter of a newborn child
The touch and love of a gentle partner
Why is it that we forget
Truly how exciting life can be

IF

If I am to be judged
By others
May they read
My words

Hear my laughter
Meet my friends and lovers
Experience the whole of me

Understand the how and why
Of what is I
Then let them judge
If they must

ONE OR FIFTY, WHICH WAY TO GO

One or fifty, which way to go
The lightness of life itself
Offering the sweet aroma of vanilla mornings
Filling our hearts and minds with newness to all
Free of all that has passed
Free of all concerns
New to every breathing living moment
Experiencing life as it offers new opportunities

One or fifty, which way to go
Is it true that being older brings more wisdom
Or is it just that new change is good
Yet change can bring new hope but also new worries
And worries seem almost too good not to experience
So is being old fear of growing outward not inward
Or is it the fear of life eroding
Slowly ending each day

One or fifty, which way to go
Will we laugh more, cry less, enjoy time more freely
Will we see sunsets and sunrises with new awareness
Will we welcome life as it happens
Facing new challenges
Facing new journeys

So is the basic truism of life
Also, the secret of life
For what life is all about
Seems so often to be
Not what is next
Not what has happened in the past
But living on and moving on

LIFE AND DEATH

Life and death have different yet same paths
My grandfather once told me "understanding life is also understanding death"
Today was one of those days
Watching the birth of a new grandson bringing bright, beautiful, new life was a joy
Meeting a nephew listening to his fight with a cancer knowing his path will have a dark end
Life and death

Two roads different paths
All the same
Life is often that way
Never just one but moments of joy and sadness
To view both is a blessing and a curse

SOMETIMES

Sometimes you hear a song that makes his memory alive again

Sometimes you find a friend that lasts forever always changing for the good

Sometimes you see a sight that echoes as an ear worm again and again

Sometimes you feel so alive that your ears dance and your soul just sings so all can hear

Sometimes you find a friend whom you love and a lover whom you discover is your best friend

Sometimes you find a book that contains words that have more meaning to you than life itself

Sometimes that song has life itself with earthly visions and words that send you soaring

SHIFTS IN TIME

Dimension shifts
Are we part of a constant string of time
Drifting between now and then
We were once there, now we are not

Different dimensions, different times
Yet some of us wonder
Do our life stories follow us
Our pain, our love, our joy, our sorrow
Or is it a new path of being
We float on by
Strings of time drifting through the endless universe

AGE

Age brings about illusions
Not all bad
Not all good
Some strangely true
Others truly strange

Age stares at you through the morning mirror
Asking who, what, why, where did that familiar person go,
It confuses you as your mind struggles to contend with memories of old friends, new friends, and current events,
Age hides beneath your compassion for others
As you ignore yourself

Age brings about fantasies
Remembering what was once
The dreams
The hopes
Past lost loves
Present love found

Age is becoming closer to reality than
you ever really wanted to be
Asking who is in control, who is not
Coming to realize that life contains time compressed
Precious seconds, minutes, hours, days, years of wonder and danger
Special times of hope and at times dread

Age waits patiently

SOMETIMES LIFE

Sometimes life seems like a great book
Full of suspense
Laughter, mystery, senseless searching for something
Looking for someone inside we connect with
Searching for truth, justice, love, hope, kindness

Abstractions in an endless circle
For it all begins and then it has an ending
Examining, reaching, drawing us in all the while

Ying and yang
Mixed reviews of right and wrong
So fast it begins
So soon it ends

Sometimes life is just a book unread

LIFE, LOVE, AND THE MEDITATION STONE

Every life has a song to sing
A story to tell
A second-by-second digital picture captured in time
A song that rises to the heavens above
So often is it not heard
And not told

Until the story itself is gone
And the story itself ends
So, the story and its song are often lost

But sometimes it lives on through the lives of others
That had life contact
With the one that was the story and the song

So, it is with the meditation stone
Quiet, solid, silent yet all-encompassing elements of life
Tightly bound in permanence
Open only to those who see
Stories revealed to a hidden touch
That takes patience to ponder the inner song

Poetry to me is never linear
It's a process of self-discovery
Much like meditating on a stone
Seeking sense of that which will never make sense
Looking inside to our soulful self
Drawing words to images
Images to thoughts
Thoughts to tummy tumbles
Connecting with our limbic pathway
Awaking our emotions deep within the amygdala
Revealing our life story
Much like mediating on a stone

NEED

Life

We think of what we need for ourselves

Step by step, year by year, we gain the knowledge of ourselves and others

School, friends, lovers, events, experiences all offer to teach us what need really means

No matter how much we learn, or where we go, or make large mistakes or small successes

We find in life, at the final stage, we always had so much more

Then we will ever need

CHANGING

Time changes us all
Years, decades, never seem that long until they are
You start at a time when breathing and moving are unique
You move on to walk and run and talk

You find life is wonderful and you are young and full of its freedom
You find love, hate, marriage, divorce, drugs, stress, and boredom
You find free will and wear it out till you're 80

You hope to find peace again
Then life changes and you look forward to just breathing

SILENCE

Silence is sometimes all you need
To establish
That solid lasting friendship
Of mind and spirit
With others and with yourself

THE MOVIE OF OUR LIVES

Sometimes our lives feel like a movie
Full of suspense
Then at times it is almost a comedy
Now and then it's a mystery
Hoping to find understanding in the script
Wondering how the ending will be

Sometimes life is a movie
Not sure of what the beginning really means
Trying to understand the true nature of the characters
Caught up in the dialogue of their daily living

Sometimes we see it in black and white
Other times full of technicolor
Always something just hidden in the background
Left to wonder what it is
How it will all wrap up
And who will be in the credits

MUSIC ABIDES

What makes your heart sing
Jazz, rock, metal, it's all there
Making your ear plugs dance
Opening your mind to a new worldview
Bringing you a natural high reaching to the sky
True peace for a worried soul
Aha, music abides

EAR WORMS

Music has always been there
Ear worms forever in my ears
Singing Latin songs as a young old choirboy

Joining my family at a drive-in movie
Listening to "rock around the clock" with Bill Haley
That's how it really started
My ears had been experiencing a new beginning
Overwhelmed
Music that flowed through you day by day

College brought me the Chad Mitchell trio
All folk songs galore Kingston Trio, Peter Paul and Mary
Philadelphia TV gave me insight to the new rock'n'roll of the late 50s

Joining the service experiencing jazz for the first time
Muddy Waters and others carried me on night by night
Vietnam embedded me with chaos listening to the Stones and the Doors
Ear worms giving my mind a rest among the craziness

Back in the world during the summer of love in San Francisco

Dancing at the Monterey Pop Festival

Janis on stage screaming in my ears forever capturing my mind

High on Boones Farm wine and local weed running among the chaos

Full of new experiences and new friends

Then surfing the beach listening to Beach Boys blaring

California dreaming driving thru laurel canyon listening to the Mamma and the Papas

Walking the stairs into the clinic at Haight and Hayes listening to the Youngbloods

Telling us all to get together

Sitting on the floor of that City Lights Bookstore learning new meanings of life

S & G demanding I listen to the silence

JT telling me I have a friend

The Dead rolling around my mind and making my ears dance

Ear worms

Where would I be without you

PART TWO: PLACES ALONG THESE PATHS

DEFINING LIFE AND LOVE WITHIN A SUSHI BAR

Defining life suddenly happens waiting in a sushi bar
Listening to the honesty of life, lies, and truth through others
Alone between two couples
Each exploring their own types of passion for each other
Is it love or is it life or is it just sex
When will it start, when will it end, together or apart
Words exchanged between bites of creatures from the sea
Exploring human passion yet hunger still abounds
They seem to be defining life thru truth and lies
Sharing that with each other is often left to secret
Where will it go from here
Aha, life and love may never offer closure
Or was it defined sitting in a sushi bar

THE TAO ROAD TO TAOS

Dark, fast-moving clouds
Drifting over the far, wide, landscape
Endlessly stretching out over the horizon
Mixing mountains, sky, and earthen pueblo's boundless beauties
Offering a shaman's view of the beginning and the end of life itself

Leaves of gold sharing space with heavy reddened rocks of ageless stone
Revealing narrow horse trails of ancient Navajo warriors
Where yataalii's sang their songs of hope and healing

Bubbling trout streams filled with silent human figures
Using bright green artificial flies attached to fancy Orvis rods
Whipping the wind with endless figures of eight
Sweeping back and forth seeking the right time and right victim

Adirondack chairs ideally waiting for golden leaves to fill them
Filling them with ghosts and memories
Of what is, what was, and what could have been

Vast open stretches where speed, wind, and horizon mesh and as one
Switchback trails that lazily weave between the mountains of stone
Calling out for walkers, stalkers, and ghosts of the past

Cooper hawks seeking dinner on the distant ground
Catching the gradient temperature shifts
Finding an opening pathway for the next thermal
Using feathery strong fingers to grasp the sky
Soaring higher and higher
Like Olympic swimmers of the sky
Patiently waiting for the next meal

Multidimensional clouds dancing amongst the bright blue sky
Violating all the rules of helium and space
Moving like the dinee of darkness surrounded within peyote dreams
Intense wild visions moving in concert with wind, sky, and land
Ageless thoughts, dreams, ghosts, and memories of new and old

Only on that Tao Road to Taos

STAR DUST

Starting late in the 40s
In the city of bridges
Home and family showing me the way
Got caught up in the sixties
Laughing loving without a moan
I floated on by

Sailed the waters from Vietnam to South America
Went to war, came home
Wondering who I was and why
Escaped anywhere there was a sea
From Panama's canal south to New Zealand
I floated on by

Began sailing thru the Virgins
Among the crystal green, blue sea
Finding a lost home on that vast voyage
Walked a crooked path thru life
Always following the horizon
And the stars
North Star, Southern Cross
Up and down
I floated on by

Walked the Rockies
Hiked the Alleghanies
Chased the Southern Star
Moved thru Asia, South American, Africa
Saw the moon as big as a city
Sitting on the mountain tops of Taos
I floated on by

Won a lifelong love with a family
Moved to the ground and never looked back
Grounded by joy, laughter, and daily love
I floated on by

Soon my soul will be star dust
Missing it all
Yet wondering if there is a solar sea
If so, I will just float on by

A LONG TABLE OF OTHERS

Our barkeep said she was closing
Yet she said OK come on in
She had us join a long table of others
She called it the last supper starting at 2 am
She said this city is a county in itself
The long table agreed

Forget the USA
Here you are who you are

She talked with a deep Irish brogue
And had a wild laugh together with pink, red streaked hair
The table held us all submerged within a sea of diversity
English songs, Dutch jokes, Irish bawdiness, Thai food,
Vietnamese beer, and Scottish curses, Czech philosophy

Each of us settled in the city by the bay
So, we closed that famous Thai restaurant down that night
Laughing and complaining about global troubles
And travels near and far
Strangers once, now all drawn together by that global bond
Life is sweet in the city by the bay

SUNSETS

I can never speak to sunsets
Out of Fear
Of losing them
For what would I do
When that special spell was gone

DON'T REALLY KNOW

Don't really know where I am
Could not really care less
Lost in a cloud of endless smoke
Just feeling down and out
Heading south on a Greyhound bus
Seems like traveling this old road of mine
Never ends
So, it becomes my lifelong job

WICHITA CITY BLUES

Walking down that long, lonely street
Feeling cold and alone in a windy winter night
Feeding on ketchup soup and free crackers
Just got a case of those Wichita city blues

Looking for the next ride out of town
The bus awaits me full of new strangers
Singing to myself as the only cure I have
Nighttime seems much darker when all you have
Is the Wichita City Blues

DAYS AND DAYS

There are days when living flows just right
Days upon days when nothing can go wrong

You sense it just waking up
Seeing some control in it all
Today just enough to make you leery

A central rhythm and theme to it all
Aha, the hidden awareness
That control is losing control
Suddenly living offers wonderful new insights

HOME

Home
I see you in the distance
Full of bright shining lights
A beacon to this speeding sailor tacking fast without a sail

Home
Never thought you would be the high desert
For this sailor's heart and mind
Always needed the sea surrounding him with a vastness embracing his being
But you opened a spot in his lonely heart of hearts

Home
The sky full of stars, endless horizons, and the ever-changing colors of the sunset
So, I set sail at night traveling by the constellations, the little dipper and Orion's belt

Then at dusk you reveal a thousand shades of blue
Combined with a clear cloudless slow enduring pink revealing my way

Home
I am glad you found me

SWARTHMORE IN FALL

A warm day with that still humid warm wind
Train horn blazing away the quiet
Wise old tree lines full of
Of Ancient old red oaks, Japanese maples and elder hickories

Line the walkways
Full of past wisdom
Filled with hundreds of years
Of secrets, past loves, youthful laughter
Silent except to the cloud filled skies
Green, green surrounds your senses

Bright full trees
Landscapes full of green
Split by splashes of bright sunlight
Dancing off the green
Old stone buildings
Stained with wonderous windows

Carefully placed political words and symbols
Mark the walkways
Speaking of peace, hope and diversity
Youthful wisdom, may they never forget

A wonderous field of roses
Red, yellow, white, pink
Offer the opportunity as a hide away
For working bees and the occasional
Student learner
Laying on the benches
Seeking the last day's sun from fall

THE HEM/ONC TRIP

Sitting in this clean
Sterile office
Waiting to be called
Waiting for fate to happen

Carefully watching those around me
Not different
Yet each living for the moment
Some with IVs hanging in the tall stands
Some wearing colorful skull caps and scarves
Some wearing the side effects of time and life

Yet there are smiles
Deep hard smiles on their faces
Speaking with their partners
Speaking to their loves
Holding hands closer than others

Questions not around today or tomorrow but the moment
So, I sit
Is this me next week, next year
Will I handle it as well?
Will I have a true companion to be there for me

Waiting for what all true companions wish for their partners
Another day, another tomorrow, another birthday

I am amazed at the courage, the honesty, the truth
Amidst all the pain, the drugs, the looming despair not spoken
They go on
So, true companions in life and beyond

Some knowing the reality of the moment
Given in birth and waiting for the recall

On the road of life
Tripping in the hem/onc office
Will it end bad or worse
Flowing with the twists and turns of hopes and wishes
All summed up on a paper green table
Listening for that endless knock on the door
...Next

LOST AGAIN IN LA

Sudden seamless realities
Of screen saver sunsets
Streaming rock and roll flowing over the sandy beaches
Human seals searching for that endless wave
Weaving in and out of the pier stanchions
Freeways over freeways
Full of tin can crazies
Hurrying nowhere
So, here it is and here I am
Lost in its unreal glitter forever

THE NIGHT MUSIC FELL FROM THE SKIES

Driving consumes my daily life
Weekends spent traversing
Mountain switchbacks through the Smokies
Radio is what keeps me awake
Endless play lists of the same tunes over and over
Dull me to sleep

So, I found the way to the circling power of music in the sky
Now my ride is filled with oldies, newies, and endless talk radio
I get no fast-food announcements, no local ads, and no chatter about new products
Just good old rock and rock, new age venues, and the blues

I can ever call up Dylan and listen to his tales of past present and future tunes
I can catch S & G, CSNY, and CCR on Deep Tracks
And soothe my soul with New Age Visions

So once again the sky is mine,
Filled with tunes to keep me company
Riding with the nighttime and real time stars
As I enter the endless switchbacks
That takes me home
Again and again on the road
With music that falls from the skies

JOURNEYS

The road of life offers many journeys
Some are crocketed
Some are narrow
Some are dangerous
Some repeat themselves
We all face the same maze of paths
Walking or running from birth till death
Wondering as life goes by decade to decade
Seeking the right path, the right answers, the right place to find
We travel the journey, yet the maze goes on
But we can always change our direction

NIJMEGEN

City of old
City of new
Bright new homes
Brilliant open people
Surround the roman cobblestones from 900 AD
Oldest city in Holland
Comfort and style ahead of its time
Built around the raging Waal River
Full of constant water traffic
Peaceful now yet prospering
In every moment

SAME STARS, SAME NIGHT

Same stars, same night
It began early in my life
Amazed at the Buhl Planetarium in the Carnegie Science Center
Looking, seeking, watching a whole new nightly world

Then Denver decades later where it seemed you could touch that sky
Milky way spread like sparkly life in the air over your outstretched hand
The new forever horizons a flood of blue night sky

Watching sunsets in Vietnam, St. Thomas, Sint Maarten and Maui
Convinces me that there is more out there than I will ever know
Orion's belt and the Dippers ever granting me the Southern Cross

Same stars, same night
Night sailing between the islands
Quiet, peaceful yet full of ocean life
Waves pushing us forward wind in our sails

Same stars, same night
From the green flash of sunset
To the falling stars at the end of the comet
To the great telescope array in the southwestern desert
We are all connected night after night
Wherever we are
All we need to do is find that
Same star, any night

CINCO DE MIO

Dreams
We all have them
Some keep us hoping
For what's next
Some Keep us awake
The what if's, guilt, worrying about needing to do
Sleep we want, we need it, it's there lost among all the worrying

Dreams
The how, when, and where
Daytime, Nighttime
Doesn't really matter
Real or imagined
I always search for meaning

Dreams
Some are empty
Many never found to be real
Others tell a story of what we lost what we want what we need
We wake seeking more of those lost stories

Dreams
The first day, the fifth day
All hopes and wishes of life
Celebration of victory over the unknown
Our very own Cinco de Mio

PART THREE:
PEOPLE WE MEET ON OUR PATHS, GUIDING US, SHOWING US THE WAY, HELPING US THROUGH THE CURVES

GREEN CHILI CHEESEBURGERS

We first met with that chance encounter
Over at the Owl Café
Rocking bar been there since the mushroom clouds covered the desert
Burger, Fries, and 60's rock and roll
Served with a smile and an iced beer

Keeping at bay the
Waves of endless heat outside
You made me smile all day
I still can taste the senses lost to hot food and too many beers
But always found with giggles from us

Burning ever so silently into our olfactory cells
Lifting our tongues to the newest of hot adventures
Never has it been replaced

So, I think time and time again
Keep searching for that Green Flash of food within my synapse
Deep within my food soul memory
Aha, green chili cheeseburgers, a cold beer and you

RAINBOW DANCER

Dancing through the stain glass cathedral rainbows
A place full of wishes, dreams, hopes and fears

Yet you dance free of it all
Rainbow dancer full of misguiding light

Trained to be a caregiver for all these things
Yet somehow you left those souls all behind
Rainbow dancer full of misguiding light
You became a user
Using the spirit of those in need

Able to use while sensing their inner most dreams, hopes and fears
Rainbow dancer full of misguiding light
Dancing around their behaviors in a slow methodical manner
Offering words without emotion

Time and time again

In and out becoming a brain worm
Leaving those wondering why
Did she do what she did
Always in control always using

Rainbow dancer full of misguiding light
Dancing through the webs of truths and lies
Saying what helps but always planning a strategy
Small but misread by all male and female

Rainbow dancer full of misguided life
Using others became a lifelong path
Avoiding your own trauma and pain
So long so far
Somehow you forgot who you are
Rainbow dancer taker of life light

MUSIC DAYDREAMS

I listen to that song
You mentioned to me about him
So long ago
Somehow it still hits me
He who was there in your heart
Before me
He who was the one who taught you
The importance of active listening to music
Feeling its deep draw to your soul
Never making you forget its value to body and mind
Strange I can still smell you there on my chest telling me the story
Me feeling so weird that I was not the one
Aha the joys and sorrows of music daydreams

MY PHYSICS DAUGHTER

She was a quiet kid
Yet always looking carefully at the motion of life
Logical to the second of sound and movement
Always offering free love
To every cat and dog alive
She is my physics daughter
Early on she had no fear
She climbed the highest tree
Practiced karate that made Rocky look weak
Became a ballerina extraordinary
Endless energy endless thinking
She is my physics daughter
She is a wonder at music
Rocking the stage with violin and flute
Making the universe move along with each note
She is my physics daughter
Soon she pursued the structure of matter
Math became her new language
The fundamental constituents of our universe
Finding it intact she turned to students
Teaching physics in a way no others dreamt
She is my physics daughter
Thermodynamics, quantum mechanics, optics, and photonics
She is logical, an incredible problem solver
Yet everyday she offers hope and understanding
To students that she shows - living is physics
In how we play
In how we work
In how we live
She is my physics daughter
And the love of my life

M

M was born in a world of chaos and strive
Raised to know right from wrong
Came to the new world
With a new beginning
Family first, family solid

M goes to the green isle
Learning the way of the old poets
Writing, living, a peaceful path
Creating words
With visions of existential thought

M leaves again for a new beginning
Providing care for others
Back to graduate school
To learn more in a 24/7 way
Gaining lifesaving skills as a PA
Feeling his way
Combining art and science to heal
So that others may live

M finds and falls out of love
Searching for self and hope
Working hard for large orgs
Only to find
Sometimes like lovers
They care more for themselves

M – he moves on to a new beginning
A new land, a new wife, a new life
Many paths, many lives, many joys
M ages well finding life, love, and passion
In work helping others help themselves
Life fills M
Peace abounds

WORDS NEVER WRITTEN

Words never written
Thoughts never shared
Emails long lost in translation
Fantasies never found
Calls never made
Thoughts drifting by
What could have been

Never written never sent
Were you ever real
Was it all your game
He wondered

As he shapeshifted emotions and dreams
Never stopping,
Just pushing the thoughts and passion

Never written never sent
Watching the sun streaming across your face
Fantasies of what could have been

Yet you always were in control
Of dreams, of hope, of possibilities
Words spoken in quiet spaces

Never written never sent
Decades passed
Lives move on
Traumas still stay real

Yours and mine aged but still present
Remaining an earworm
Life paths moved us separate ways, separate lives
You, now most powerful and secure in your fame
Me, just managing to make it through day by day
Thoughts drift by on sunny days
Decades of finding peace and love from others
Words
Never written never sent

MY PUZZLE QUEEN

As she looks over the table
1000, 500 pieces of life that tell the story
Story lines mixed with fun, family, love, and life
Small, jarred pieces all mixed
Begging to be put together
Carefully she watches

Logically she places each piece
As a part of life
Needing the right love
The right motion, the right connection, the right color
Just like life itself

First the border around the art
Which like life is the story of the beginning and the end
Then she divides the colors and pieces each with their meaning
Over and again each to their assigned places

Till all the connections come together
Carefully and thoughtfully
As she does with her friends and family
Ever so caring ever so thoughtful

Mother, daughter, wife all intertwined pieces yet connected
She is the puzzle queen
Both on paper and in life
Bringing it all together
No matter how ontological it ever is
Her logic drives her forward

Caring for all
Wishing the best
Making us all just a little better
More connected and together
Just like her puzzles

A GOOD MOTHER

So why do I know you're a great mother?

Because I watch you hold her for dear life as she views the world in wonder

Because I see the way you speak to him with respect and kindness

Then I see the way you make them both giggle

And the way you fill them with love every day, beginning to end

And I see the way you handle the frustration of being a mom – some days are good, and some are just ugly, yet you struggle to remain calm

But I watch you discipline with firmness yet kindness of spirit and always focusing on improvement

Then I watch how your eyes go soft and you relax as you watch them giggle and catch each other around and around

So how do I know?

It's the way your love reaches out in a smile, a giggle, a round of laughter, a rapid check on their care

The comfort of your hugs, the way you are with each of them individually

Even when I see the chaos building but hear the calmness in your voice never condemning always encouraging

So all in all I know you are a great mom, because every day, every way you try to do your best by them

you do your best by the sounds in your heart and the belief of God as your teacher

They are your heart and soul, your love, your joy and at times your sorrow

Good job, my love

ENABLERS

Some tread softly in the shadows of our thoughts
Others dance in the cathedrals of our feeling leaving behind rainbows

Some are tall and loud
Some are small and wise
Some offer a new vision of the way out of the box
Others push us beyond the context of our self-imposed limits and theories

Some are beyond the phenomenological side of life
Others slide along the straight and narrow
Some come quietly into our lives
Others leave large footprints in the sands of our soul

Some give us vision
Others give us hope

Some bring us together with our touch
Others leave their touch on us

Some are teachers of the soul
Others are teachers of lifelong yearning

ALWAYS

Always
There in my heart and mind
Rivers, mountains, and islands
Never far away
No matter where I go
Near and far
At sea or on ground
You are forever around me
Always in my heart and mind

THE PADDLE

She always had a paddle
Stuck in her trunk
Just in case
She spoke
I am up the creek without one

So it went
She was the true half of Thelma and Louise
Running free without conditions

First a scientist nerd
Then a stern psychiatric nurse

Running free from it all
In her thirties off to roam
China, India, Vietnam, Laos, Brazil
Free spirit extortionary

Traveling on a whim just going
Capturing it all on thousands of Kodachrome slides
Forever shown by carousel on the wall
Of her cabin in the woods

She left life as she found it
Free and wondering where she would go next
Yet never ever up a creek without a paddle

I HAVE BEEN LUCKY

I have been lucky
You as my other half for more than 40 years
Not always agreeing
Not always clear
Not always together

But I have been lucky
For when you are near
My life has greater meaning

Your smile and laugh
Still make my ears dance
And my heart soar

You have touched my deepest soul
With a simple hug
You know I love you

But do you know how safe you make me feel
For I am lucky
To have found you
A friend
A family
A lover
I have been lucky

DAVE AND THE GOLDEN BRIDGES

He grew up top of the city hillside
Watching the city of golden bridges grow
He survived hard times

Emotionally falling in love and life
So he found a new road
He kept reinventing himself

He had grown up with a tough crowd
All working hard to survive
In the city of golden bridges

He wondered what to do
Among the throngs of those living for survival
Drugs, crime, poverty
He fought to be better
He kept reinventing himself

So, he worked under the golden bridges
Hanging in a bosun chair
Watching the rivers building lengths below
Working with a gang of Greek, Polish, and Russian painters
Learning to swear in each language
Seeing life and death at a moment's notice
All hoping like him
To reinvent themselves

He started a band
Rock and Roll was his path
He could repeat Dylan's lyrics in his sleep
Finding himself thru those words
Over and over again

He kept reinventing himself
He went to college
Where he became a wizard
His star was chemistry
Components and tables dancing in his head
Like music only clearer

He kept reinventing himself
He moved west for forty years
Helping those who helped others
Making it safe to fix those high electric wires
Keeping those electric dancers alive
He kept reinventing himself
He found himself helping others live

CATCH AND RELEASE

He grew up smiling and giggling at his grandma's fish tank
Always trying to reach the fish
Those days he never had a bad day

Tried to be a field star running fast and kicking soccer balls
Fought stick to sticks in La Crosse, wrestled till he almost fainted
Found himself in grappling
Focusing on the next match
Judo was his thing
Strengthen his body and his mind

Then one day he caught his first fish
No talent, no skill, just luck
So it began
Catch and release
Bass, trout, salmon, perch, pike
From then on, he never met a stream of water he didn't like

Ponds, rivers, creeks, lakes, and oceans
All keepers for his search for freedom
Learning to adapt and overcome this new task as he did all others
New rods, new reels, tying flies that were more real than nature itself
As in judo he sought the secret of the search knowing there was a symmetry to it all
Knowing when and where to wait
Knowing how to sit patiently until the strike

Today as a grown man he still lives for the hunt
Catch and Release
Telling each catch he is grateful
To simply be their fisherman

GOODBYE

Why did I ever say goodbye
Knowing I had let so much of me go with you

SO MUCH ALIKE

You and I are so much alike
So very mad in our separate lives
We play the game of life
Floating around alone
Holding onto others for comfort and support
We give so little of ourselves and expect so much of others
Some would say we take more than we ever give
The both of us so bold, so untrue to our real selves

What are we afraid of
Loss, Gain, Love, Life, Harmony?
We seem to thrive in our sadness using it to feel sorry for our selves
We seek reassurance, love, and renewal from others

Can anyone really know who we are
Why are we searching so aimlessly for ourselves
We hide in the habit of being in love
Without knowing what it is
Or how fulfilling it can be for two
You and I are so much alike
Alive but not knowing the reality of living

ALSO

Also, let us choose the time we spend
Together as ourselves
Rather than in-between other times
In other words, as our own time
And let the affection we show
Express only what is between us
Concurrently with ourselves
Not displaced energy from somewhere else
Without that being understood
How can there be honesty among us

BEDTIME

I miss you
At night
Talking to that empty
Side of the bed
Winding down the day
Where did you go?
I miss you
Rolling over
Sensing your warm side
Waiting for me
I miss you
Nightly!

MY BROTHER, THE MENSCH

He spent more than 30 years of his life
Caring for so many
The needy, the poor the underserved
He faced the giant demons of politics and evil narcissists
And stood against them all
With his own deep-rooted sense of solid compassion
Built on personal integrity
With a rare sense of honor

Doing the deed for the right reason
Always asking why not rather than how much
His endless caring made a difference
For the young   the old   the dying   as well
He was a listener comforter to all
He rarely slept through the night
Worrying about how can he save more lives tomorrow

Never seeing an importance in his titles or citations
Knowing everyone from floor cleaners to surgeons
Saying hi every day to all
Steadfast in lasting humanistic values and sustainable health for all
So now his life shadow is growing shorter

He wonders about tomorrow
When will it all end and what will it all matter
Was it a good life?

Yet there in the distant shadows of eternity
There are a thousand voices
A million souls

Screaming out "you made a difference
for each of us"
Someday in the far-off clouds
He will hear as he passes
There goes a real mensch
So it goes for my brother of another mother

JERRY, THE SEADOG

There are those who walk differently in life
Smelling salty seas miles away
Having visions of endless fantail swells
Standing true in the sucking wind on the forecastle
Watching the horizon for land's highest point
Listing port and starboard with each huff of wind
Seeking that lighthouse of life offering forever
guidance against the rocks of daily life
Watching the sun rise at the break of a new morning
With a strong coffee in hand
Awaiting the joy of another day – another port – another time
Seadogs forever even when landlocked

HE KEEPS ON TRYING

He gave up trying
When he watched his grandmother die in an oxygen tent within the crowded living tomb of a poor hospital ward

He gave up trying
When his mother died after her third heart operation

He gave up trying
When he listened to this brother's final Cheyne-Stokes breath ending the struggle with AIDS

He gave up trying
To surround himself with the peacefulness of knowing and accepting a higher power

He gave up trying
To remember the intensity of spiritual oneness of innocence
He held as a young altar boy filled with hope

He gave up trying
To focus on that centered calmness of self he found alone so high in the clear, clean, Rocky Mountains of the 70's

He gave up trying
To understand the loss of friends and family he suffered through human tragedy – war, disease, stress, and lack of hope

He keeps on trying
To find and be the humanist he feels deep down in his inner soul

He keeps on trying
God Keeps on Laughing

FRIENDS OR LOVERS

Perhaps to choose one's friends
Is more essential
Than choosing lovers
Friends tend to last longer

CONNECTIONS

Through life we look for and find connections
Some with instant meaning
Others that appear through a haze distant but there
All too often we focus just on people connections
Who, why, what do they need or expect
We forget everything else that connects
Nature, life, places, loves, tribes, hate, wars, peace, time
All of these have meaning
It's up to us to look for and find their meaning
How do they connect
How do we connect
How don't we connect
Why is that

BARB, MY TRUE EARTH MOTHER

Back in the day you kept me sane when all around me wasn't.

And your endless wisdom gave me a sense of peace and hope.

Remembering all the great free meals I got with lots of communal laughter.

Because of you as our center I was always filled with laughter, giving me a continuous smile and making me think outside of my square box – thank you my earth mother

WEIRD

I listen to that old song
Hearing your voice filling my soul
Knowing it came from him
Remembering how you mentioned him to me

You said he was the one on that true path
So long ago, still right today

Somehow it still hits my soul
He who was there before me
In your heart and soul
Showing you that life path
Teaching you to sing and play from your heart
You feeling each song deep in your soul

I still remember you telling me this story
Laying on my chest
Me feeing weird that I was not the one
That had made that connection for you
Now it's just a daydream of the weird
As I watch the world chase you
So I wonder did you ever find your true path
Will we connect again
On these wide and winding paths of life

THE MUSE

We all have need of our muses
Some high sparkling in the night
Some that walk by our side
Both good and bad

We all have need of our muses
Some are tall and speak forever
Some are small and barely speak a word
Some seem to forever stare yet never speak

We all have need of our muses
For me it was all of you
Full of joy and hutzpah
Never without a word
Always there with kindness

We all have need of our muses
Left alone would I have been so driven
Would I still be waiting for something to happen
Seeking direction to some lost scared path

We all have need of our muses
All of you gave the wakeup call
Do it, do it now
Look deeper
Keep writing
Seek more, be more
So it goes
And I am forever grateful

TO A LONG-LOST SON

Long lost son
You were there during such times of chaos
Both of us thought we were so young and free
Both dealing with inner pain and self-searching
Your father struggling with the past
Your mother living to be needed, hoping for a home
Both needing safety, security, and stability

You came about through a love of two lost souls
Both misguided and misdirected
Right, wrong, complex, confused

Yet don't ever think you were not loved
The day you were born there were smiles and laughter everywhere
Even in your soft, small body, you smiled at us both
Yet the time was not right

So, you went away to another family
And as time went on we did too
We both found our separate families of new
Sons, daughters, years past

Yet you were never forgotten
We always wondered about your unknown
Even birthday in May we think of you
Wondering what could have been

Years later we all met again
Finding what some call closure
Learning more about each of our separate stories
I rest easy knowing you are well and happy
Now the universe seems all in the right place
But at times I still find this strong sense of wonder
Our paths separated then crossed
Life is so connected in so many ways of wonder

MY FAVORITE COOKIE

You are like my favorite ever cookie
It looks so good
Black and white
Tasting even better

It gave me a taste of wonder
That sense of newness
First ever cookie
First ever love

A taste that can never be forgotten
Never just one taste
But followed by many others
Yet so fearful of each second bite
Will it be the same
With other lovers

But the second third and last
Just seemed to always get better
Just like being with you

THE SPIRIT RIDER

She represents years of smiles that bring simple joy
Smart as a whip from the day she was born
Always letting you know when she was happy
Always letting you know when she was not

Watching her grow was a joy
Full of somersaults and giggles
She always climbed high
The higher the better
Never an ounce of fear

Her life of music started with the piano
Soon after she conquered the tuba
Making it's music fill the air inside and out

Her safe place is around a stable
Best if its full of horses
She never met a horse she would not hug
She developed that rider's ageless seat when she was small
Her spirit and the horse became one

Riding horse's hands over her with full confidence
Always in charge
Today she grows so much taller
Older and wiser
But still the best hugger of horses ever
And so much stronger
Nothing ever stops her
Once her mind says go
She is in charge

A forever friend, full of honor and integrity
Yet still searching for her true self
I only wish I could still be there with her
Never to guide, never to show her a right path
Just to know her as she faces each fork in the road
Ten or twenty or thirty years from now
As she rides that inward spirit forward
As she rides on

OLD FRIENDS

We sit side by side
Aware of how long we have done this
Listening and laughing to and at each other
Knowing what life has brought us
And how we have lived that life
Understanding the best in each other
Accepting who we are for what we are
We talk of yesterday
We listen to each other about today
How nice it is to be with someone who understands
Our secrets, our truths, our dreams, our wishes
Silence, laughter, fears, and old age aches
Peace and love
Old friends
What a pair

EPITAPH

People look and say
What's changed
You seem so different
Not so serious
Not so lost

People listen and say
You look different
You sound different
What happened

People listen and say
You seem so sure
You seem so secure
You seem so centered

People listen and say
Why, how, and when
You just say I found my Aha!
Another day has begun
Filled with the epitaph of what life is
Hope

FACE FIX

Often in the late evening
I find that I need a face fix
Your face fixes it all
Times your face comes alive in my hands
Knowing every bone muscle sigh and smile

So I find myself thinking
Of all those peaceful times
When I find myself watching you sleep
Watching you talk
Noticing small simple smiles that glow

Now in the daytime
I find myself watching your smile
Finding a sense of quiet and peace within

And at times
I reach up and touch your smile
Feeling that inner warmth
The sense of love it gives my soul
And when I am away from you
Late at night
Oh how I long for that face fix

YOUR SENSE OF MEANING

You find yourself remembering the times in life when you questioned yourself
"Am I good enough, am I happy enough, am I rich enough"
Wondering why life is so full of unknowns and perilous side roads
The quest always seems to be why when and how come
Sometimes the answers are simply driven by the instinct of survival
Sometimes the answers take lifetimes to find

You find yourself remembering the times in life when meaning was found just living
Witnessing a new beginning
Finding a love that lasts longer than you thought
Laughing with your friends in the family
Enjoying a discussion with friends over the secret of life
The quest keeps taking me down different roads

Sometimes the answers come so fast we miss them
Sometimes the answers come in one quick emotional orgasm
Sometimes there are too many to understand
So we are left with just more questions

PART FOUR: THOSE WHO PROVIDE SERVICE ABOVE THEMSELVES

VETERANS

Long ago we all went to war
Now we walk in silence back in the world
Some say we carry sins of that chaos
But we know the true meaning of chaos
We know all about survival
Others only think they know

War leaves you alone
Without your squad, your team, your people
Filled with lonely sleepless nights
Cold sweats in snowy winter
Bitter memories of friends
And sisters and brothers lost
Always the question of why

We are not strangers to meaningless silence
Neither are we friends of the horror of war
Been there,   done that,   we keep it deep inside
War never leaves us

Warrior scars have aged us beyond our physical age
Some show and some never will locked deep within our psyche
So we walk the walk about the granite
Seeing others looking the same
Sisters and brothers of other mothers together again
All having memories burning behind our eyes
Seeing that stone that could be us
Wondering why not me

Some of us are like the walking dead
Warriors alone like all past and future warriors
Each living with our ghosts
Some real, some friendly, some scary, some calling out our name

We have seen life and liberty as a fragile nanosecond
So we cherish every moment of every day that we breathe free
Forever looking over our shoulders
For others that were left behind
Looking at names in granite never forgetting

SURVIVOR

I came back
I survived
I endured
I am here today

But will I survive myself
The dreams
The ghosts
The thoughts
The fears
The presence of others lost long ago
The memories meant to be left behind

But will I survive my self
Only if I let myself ask for help

GOING BACK

There is no going back
Time doesn't work that way
At least not in this dimension

Nor does life
We have our day to day
Hours to hours
Moment to moment

Yet we never can return to that long-lost time zone
That day so real, so perfect
That life, so good, so remembered as memories take over
Lost forever, but not really gone

So, find value in your time now
It won't be here forever
We can never go back
But we can go forward

WILL YOU REMEMBER MY NAME

Will You Remember My Name
Or just my loss
Your brother, sister, father, son, lover
I was there for you, for country, for others

Doing what I could, never perfect
Being the best that I could be
Will You Remember My Name

Have you said it out loud lately
Does my picture sit on the nightstand
Don't worry, I am always there
Will You Remember My Name

Laughing, loving, happy and full of life
Knowing you were the life of my life
Will You Remember My Name

So, think of my service
To you, to others, to my mates
Let that thought linger
Just for awhile
Today and tomorrow
Just Remember My Name

AN EIGHTY-YEAR-OLD MAN

There are times when I see
Myself
As an eighty-year-old man
Within this thirty-year-old body
I have lived, loved, and laughed at myself
Touched death so close as to feel it's cold damp breath on my soul
Witnessed and held my daughter in my arms
Only to see her lost to a far-off war
Like the one I experienced so long away

I have lived with the guilt of living while knowing others have died
Seeing them often late at night in the mist of my dreams
I have held life in my hands and watched it disappear
Wondering what I should have or could have done to prevent it
It was always a time for tears never wept

Crying for the living that should have died
And the dead that should have lived

Yet I have known the love of a family
The lifelong love of a woman
The love of my children that warmed my heart and cleared my head
So I sit here with my eighty-year-old mind
Lost somewhere in my thirty-year-old body
Wondering what will be next

The sorrows of yesterday and thoughts of today
Moving on to the hopes of tomorrow
Will I have the strength of mind to continue to move forward
In an eighty-year body with a thirty-year-old mind?

MEMORIAL DAY

Long ago we went to war
Today we walk slowly back in the world
They all say "Thank you for your service"

Trying but not knowing what else to say
Yet few will ever really understand
Because we carry our war and survival alone

We miss it, we hate it, we gave it our all
War leaves you alone
Without a team

Filled with sleepless nights,
cold sweats in summer
and bitter memories of friends
brothers and sisters lost
Yet we are not strangers to meaningless silence
Our ghosts are always there to remind us
They quiet in the mist so we stay quiet
In our selves
Knowing that to speak the reality of our dreams
Is to be labeled unwell
Warrior scars have aged us beyond our physical age
Some show on our bodies
And others are deeply hidden in our psyche
Yet we are the lucky ones
So we gather
Brothers and sisters together again
Jungle, Sand, and Rockpile memories burning behind our eyes
Deep within our souls decades later

We talk quietly
We hug fiercely
We look for those who have fallen
In graveyards on the web on the memorial walls
And we try to help ourselves
Understand
Why are the walking dead?
We are the warriors
Alone like all past and future warriors
Living with our ghosts
Some friendly, some caring, some scary
We who have seen life and liberty
Know it as a fragile nanosecond
So, we honor every day and every moment we breathe free
And forever look over our shoulders
For all the others left behind
And those in our souls never left behind

WHEN DARKNESS LOOMS

When it's dark and gloomy in this old man's head
Remembering times of war, pain, and suffering
He wonders about life and what's to come

He finds fresh amazement at the beauty of a month-old baby girl sleeping on his chest
Encompassed in that beautiful hair and feeling life fill her chest against his
He takes endless joy in simply watching his three-year-old grandson chase his dog's tail
While never stop giggling as the chase goes on

He finds solitude in knowing at times like these, life cannot be better
And he owes it to so many who helped him go on

He finds the secret of living in simply knowing
That chosen and given family are there
And it makes him smile knowing life is so real and precious,
For all these things and more he is grateful to be alive
Even when darkness looms

VAN, AGAIN

Well it's been a long time
There you lie peaceful at the end
Finally finding peace, minus that great smile

What a life you had, full of rage and thunder
How you laughed at it all
Then a quiet calm
After the fame

Dying of nanoparticles left from the war
You were the seminal woman of that war
Everyone who hated you then
Talks about how much they love you now
Funny I can't see you smiling

You told the truth
But no one wanted to hear
So you were threatened
Left alone, ostracized by all

You got sober, married, again
But this time for real and good
Blessed with a great family
And a wonderful daughter

You gave them both your entire heart and soul
So, it worked for many years
Back to work as a nurse
Back to life as an author
Writing war poetry
Second to Sassoon

So, there you lie
Thousands walking by
Offering their good words
Large pictures of your life filled with spirit and strength
They surround your casket

So, I hear them say quietly thank you
Mostly to themselves can you hear them
What a life you had
We will miss you
Your vision, your strength, your passion, and your laughter
You won your wings
Keep watch for us all in the stardust

BROTHERS AND SISTERS IN GRANITE

Stone cold, yet always here
As we touch their names
We hear them in the stardust stream of life
Laughing, talking, crying, screaming
It changes with all our moods
They go on living a life many forgot
We go forward saying their name
Yet never forgetting their service above self
Names, numbers, numbness
Ghosts that forever haunt us
Making us laugh making us cry
Making us ask why
Why them not me
They are not in stone
To us they are life stories
Often told with humor
Often remembered with sadness
Now we can only call out their names
Touch their souls in stone
Place a stone or coin or medal in honor
Yet they are always – Present
Brothers and sisters, known and unknown
Brothers and sisters in Granite
Not ever gone,
Just waiting to say welcome

LIFE SAVERS THEN....
CAREGIVERS FOREVER

It was a night full of hero stars – bronze, silver, gold – that lit up the room
Visions past, present and future
Heroes walking new and old
Some in uniform
Some seeing themselves in uniform of old
Memories of Friends, comrades, soulmates filled the room

So there stands a soldier tall in army brown
Once a gentle medic, lugging his comrades on his shoulders
Far above the erupting ground of death
Doing his best under the worst of conditions
Trying wishing with all he had
That he could have known more – might have been more
All he could offer was presence, pressure, patience, promises and prayers
But when it came time to save those under his care
He never gave up, doing all he could and more

There stands a navy corpsman wearing her FMF badge shining brightly
Once she was shrouded in Marine Corp green
Corpsmen up rising to meet the call giving the kiss of the angels
Offering lifesaving breaths while whispering words of comfort
Listening for sounds of life whispering words of hope,
While bullets seem to float by as sounds of death surrounded her
Offering herself and at times her soul as protector for her Marines
They saw her as confessor sister savior and keeper of life

There stands that Air Force PJ, quietly taking it all in
Once adored in jolly jungle green
Trained to do what most others only dream about
Focusing on the mission at hand
Living up to the motto "that others may live"
Offering service about all including self
Not fearing what others dread but living for the odds
Prepared for the worst yet always hoping for the best

So here they are now
RNs NPs PAs EMTs MDs, healers all
Life savers confessors of the living and comforters of the dying
Putting themselves in harm's way
Offering hope with morphine to ease the pain
And silent quiet prayers to a higher power for one last hope
Older but second to none
Offering caregiving   heart saving   life making with respect and compassion
That only those who have been among the thousand-yard stares
Will ever really know
They always think of the living, yet they still dream of the sick and dying
They appreciate and know the preciousness of life
Knowing more than most about the secret of life
Its second-by-second meaning
Linking forever past with present
Lessons learned in the forgotten fogs of war
For they are now and forever will be
Life Savers then.... Caregivers Forever

MY RETURN

Fifty years have passed yet was it not yesterday
Was I ever really that young?
So here he stands many decades later
Surrounded by those he was with day after day
Brothers of a different family yet still connected
Same ghosts, same fears, same dreams
Living through the traumas of those chaotic days
Not knowing if the next day would be the last one
Or would it be today?
Who is next?
So, we each bring our ancient baggage still intact
Seeing through that current face knowing a younger one
How will we be received?
Do we really want to be here
Do we really want to remember?
As we talk and share our worldviews of old and new times
We see the war from a new perspective
We talk about the good times
Quietly we also talk about the bad times
Slowly our shared ghosts seem to become less real
Strange to be here
As if it never ended
Yet now it feels like a different safe place
Feeling shared laughter and thoughts and dreams
Both good and bad
Brotherhood is such a unique dimension
It makes you feel you belong
Making you feel together again

SO IT BEGAN

"Be careful he's violent"
She said as I was told to care for him
Boats, he was my first patient
Learning by doing everything new and real
So I approached
Thinking about what my nurse had said
So it began

There he was in a Navy-blue patient coat
Looking angry sitting in an old wheelchair full of faded patches
IV's in both arms, foley bag on the side of his one leg
Arms and neck full of withering story tattoos
A large red W. C Fields nose full of old scars
So it began

I watched and read this man as a testimony to the old salt motto
Clearly he was old Navy   been there   done that
First person I ever met that could swear twenty words in one sentence
He was a testimony to living fast in many different lives all over the globe
Now he was in dry dock never to sail again
So it began

Every day we never talked much just small talk
I asked if I could get him something
He asked for magazines cigarettes candy
I smuggled it all in and slowly asked him about him
So it began

Our next days were slowly filled with his stories as we went outside
He would sit on the lawn smoking while watching the ocean
Looking for a way out a way to sail on
So it began

I learned stories of him as boat coxswain under fire living a life unknown to many
He was a Chief Boatswains Mate working on every type of ship in the fleet
I listened to stories of WWII carrying troops to islands leading to Japan
Chopping ice from patrol boats in Korea
Working as an advisor on the rivers of Vietnam
So it began

I spent the three weeks caring for him
He was my most important patient
Teaching me to listen never to judge
Understanding the pain and anger of loneliness
Seeing pain tear down the end of living - he died alone and sad
So it ended

GOD LOVES THE GRUNTS

He spent years in the jungle
Got wounded three times
Medals, promotions praise for all for his service
Returning home, he hoped to make it to twenty
The system said thanks, but you seem "not right"

So he found himself in his painting
First it was sunsets that captured light, long lost spirits, and beauty
Then the sadness hit home
Remembering his thousand-yard stares
Never ending just hidden behind his eyes

So he painted his sorrows being wounded
Seeing the war as others could not image
Telling the story of the men and women behind those memories

So it was
Painting that grunt on the ground
Looking through you with those thousand-yard eyes
Surrounded by thousands of signatures
Honoring that person they resembled so long ago
Veterans looking for friends brothers and sisters
Never missing in their lives yet lost so long ago

So it goes
Each knowing that image said it all
Been there done that still remember it all late at night
The artist warrior never imagined how big a treasure it was

God Loves the Grunts because no one else does

WALL OF NAMES

They all came that first day in March 1982 wondering how it would go
Dry cold filled the air, seemingly appropriate for that day
Standing in that long V shoulder to shoulder with a shovel
Friends and families gathered around
Photographers ready with their cameras waiting for something to happen
Then they dug, turning the dirt over carefully knowing what it would be
Breaking ground on a future wall of remembrance a place of pain and suffering
Yet a place of brothers and sisters lost forever in the war
So it was built with black marble standing tall

It was raised in November another very dry and cold day

Vets filled the space overwhelming the ground above and below the memorial

Some even climbing the surrounding trees just to see a name a part of their inner soul

Always looking for that special one a name with a memory left far away

As it went up many were angry

They said "it's dark, it's black, it's in a trench, it only has names"

Yet once it stood there it drew your reflection in the solid blackness

Giving it a sense of time long ago

Stories never told sorrows never forgotten

Ghosts that seem to be still within our souls

Now always there a real source of our own space and time

Long ago but still packed in our hearts and minds never to be forgotten

Forty years ago it was raised

Just sharing a name in marble along with self-reflections holding a life lost story

Started with a vision to never forget, the sacrifice the service the brotherhood

Becoming a place of remembrance

A place where those who fought could always recall those who stood beside them

Standing 500 feet in length, 10 feet tall
Chiseled in remembrance
The average age of twenty-three years of young lives lost
Over 58,000 others representing the circle of that war
Its beginning and its end for those from our shores
Hallowed ground that reflects and contemplates
A sacred place
Today those that visit never forget the walk among those lost together
Leaving more than 400,000 pieces of memories simply saying we never will forget
This wall of names and the stories deep within our souls

WALKING DEAD

We are the walking dead
Long ago in jungles far from home
Our sons and daughters now
Serving on the rockpile and in the sand

We were exposed
Agent orange, white, blue and green
Vietnam Laos Thailand
Diabetes   lymphoma   leukemias   amyloidosis
Multiple myeloma   parkinson's   neuropathy
Making us the walking dead

My kids now face the same yet different
Burn pits   oil wells   toxic air
Bahrain   Iraq   Afghanistan   Yemen   Syria
Chronic fatigue   fibromyalgia   irritable bowel
They too will be the walking dead

Chemicals radiation warfare air pollutants
All in the mix
We served our country
Will our country serve us?

PART FIVE: THOSE THAT CARE FOR OTHERS

PA'S WE ARE

Not a doctor not a nurse
But a PA
Always the same question
When are you going to be a doctor

Physician Associates we are
Coming together in a diverse different class of health care providers
Experienced as military free clinic workers Women's Health leaders
From day one we learn to be patient centered listening and acting

Striving for excellence every day
Inspiring each other to learn more
Functioning on a fire hose of medical information every day
Dreaming of notes and lessons
Cramming four years of medicine in half the time

We all learned how why and when to do our best
We all learned our limits from day one
We were the best that we could be
Striving for knowledge
Learning how to learn rapidly
Caregivers all

So it started
Mentored and challenged each day
Together we survived struggling yet gaining on new challenges
Never ending information lifelong learning ahead
Learning medicine and learning life
Chasing horses not medical zebras
Understanding compassion and caring as lifelong skills

Together we began
Together we finished
Fifty years later
We are all still in the game
In every medical specialty
Throughout the globe
Caring teaching passing on what we know

PA's we are

HIS LAST BREATH

There he lies
Forty years young
Dying from a DCI side effect
Back in the 80s
When finite care was unresolved

Cheyne-Stokes breaths
Rising and falling like his sailboat
At the mooring in the sound
Eyes forever moving in painless REMS
Consciousness lessened
By the endless drip of morphine

Years as a sailor had leathered his face
Months of AIDS had taken its weight
He lies there
Riding the crest of each breath

Brother of mine
Lost to us both
So long ago
Yet never far away from the phone
And words of renewal

There I was watching the end
Wishing we had more time more connections with each other
The way we were before
Years ago, me his Big Brother
Trying hard to defend him against all odds

But in the end
What could I do
But sit and watch and try to understand
His last breath

RUTH, THE CHANGE AGENT

She was a social worker in the beginning
Raised by a father who was an airborne healer

She re-invented herself as a MEDEX health provider for those in need
Working especially with young women helping every way she could
Making and getting involved with change was her mantra
Organizing committing to a needed cause volunteering to do more

She was always there working to find solutions and change
Never an easy woman but then brilliant, smart, strong women never are
She worked endlessly for change in all aspects of health care

Traveling the world speaking on behalf of those in need
Always on the forefront of each global committee
Adding what others never thought of
Bringing her social studies forever into play

Never asking "what if" but always asking "why not"
She wrote, spoke, taught, and mentored thousands
Never missing a beat when it came to helping others
Honored by her profession but forever seeing more to do
You will be missed and remembered by more than you ever expected

BYPASS NEXT DAY

"Alive, my God, am I still alive
Or am I?"

I hear the EKG noisily beeping
I know that sound

OK which side of the bed am I on
My synapses scramble to understand

Four hours of surgery
Cocktails of drugs swirling in my soul
Making each nanosecond both psychotic and psychedelic
Aha, that lifesaving beeping
So goes the rhythm of life

Floating in and out
Making the "Dude's" trip seem real

Yea I made it
Now what
No bright lights leading the way
Just time to be again
Mental promises bucket lists people to see places to visit
Finding who I am again and what my worldview will be

Promises to stay closer to life family and friends
Hopes to be better at life this time
Nice to have another chance
At reinventing myself
This time I will do it right??

PATIENT ADVOCATES

My grandmother laying in a long room of patients
Breathing inside a tent of oxygen to stay alive
One of fifty in a long hospital ward
Even then as a young boy I wondered why it could not have been better

We all go in the future not knowing where our roads will take us
Some of us find we are committed to caring for others
In the sixties some of us went in the military offering ourselves for others
Caring for those that served more than most
Our paths led from running in ambulances to floor nursing
Then learning how to help others learn as educators
Some became Physician Associates (PA)

Patients always asked when will you be a real doctor
We always say no we are PAs
PAs are the best thing that happened to Vietnam Veterans returning to care for others
Now we are traveling around the world
Mayors in major cities
Starting health care systems
Building free clinics mobile van
Offering global advocacy for others health
Making health care access and delivery face to face over the net
Being there during hard times even when pandemics gave new daily challenges
Always focusing on our limits
Forever being a class of overachiever's
All working together in a team to make sure we can offer the best

Looking back over fifty years we are not perfect

But we are excellent

Every day PAs strive for excellence in providing care and compassion

Never giving up

Just giving more

We stand on the shoulders of those medics and corpsmen veterans before us

Giants who broke the mold delivering family practice health care in urban and rural areas

We make a difference no matter where we go or what we do day in day out

Listeners, caregivers, counselors, educators, healers all

PA - Physician Associate/Patient Advocate

AND THEN THERE WERE ANGELS

Those crazy rock - and - roll times
When life moved fast though life
Pain suffering happiness, joy all in an eye blink
Like that sixty-second flash of video

Watching it begin and end in a nanosecond of eternity
Sensing angels somewhere in that peripheral vision

The sight of life itself
A sight that seems to speak out loud
Slow down
Find your quiet time be peaceful
Examine what you have
Stop and feel life itself
Enjoy the moment
Enjoy the day
Find some goodness
Reach out to others
Feel alive

And as quickly as the vision appears
It disappears
And then there were angels no more

WHY DO YOU DO WHAT YOU DO

This question seems to have followed him for over 40 years
Perhaps that's when it started
A second chance given by an angel
Long ago yet yesterday
He jumped into the early dark morning of a place far away
Razor grass cutting into his soul
Air full of thick humid molecules of fear

He came swiftly, silently
Moving arm to elbow hip to hip inch by inch
Then the world erupted into a chaos of hurt and pain
Letting him fly up like superman then down like he hit a solid brick wall

Nano centuries later an angel with a green face came to drag him back in time itself
That angry angel of the night screaming yelling   dragging him back on his life force
Maybe that is when the question began
Payback

The question got darker 20 years later
For on that brilliant sunny peaceful California day
He stood looking into that dark deep hole
Watching the red   white   blue colors and stars folded over that long box
The angel had swallowed a 357 ounce of lead freeing his pain
But not his soul
So many owed him their lives, their futures
He wanted to scream and shake that fallen angel back to life

He was ready to surrender all that he ever held dear

Instead, he found himself high on a beach cliff ready to scream at the world

Instead, he found someone lying at the base of the cliff

Leaking their life in the spider streams that fed the sea

Now he became the angel stopping the bleeding and giving breaths of life

All the while feeling another presence next to him

Telling him do it quickly   do it how you were taught   make it right   call for help

After that the question was answered and help arrived

Call it caring!

Call it compassion!

The angel knew the truth

Never letting anyone forget it

Whenever having self-doubts, he again found his angel among others in the gardens of stone

Forever talking to this angel about that payback a time long ago

He feels blessed having an angel and a lifelong ghost that keeps him on the path

Who got him to do

What he did for forty years

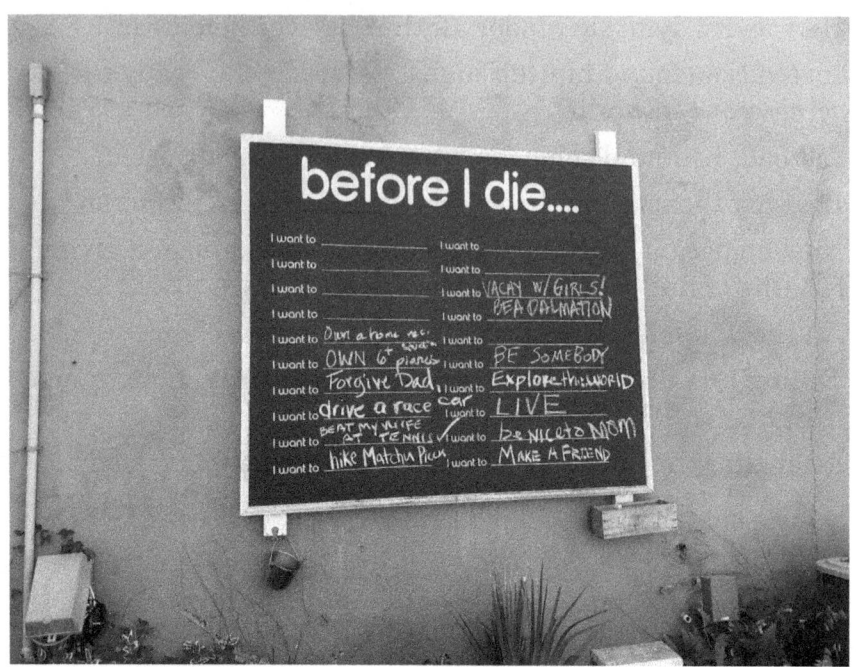

LIFE MEETS DEATH

Life begins before we ever are aware
Yet at times our tiny bodies explore it with a giggle
Seeming to know its meaning
Life meeting death

We grow and move through our existence
Family School Life
She went to war and she was lucky
She learned the true value of life
Learning the fast way watching others die slowly fast
Both physically and mentally
Quiet screaming scared, painful
Life meeting death

She became a caregiver
Again watching life overcome by death
Saw children die around her soon to be daughter
They went noisily wondering why
She came through stronger than ever
Life meeting death

She continued to care for so many
Code teams trauma teams masses of caregivers all trying to stop death
Mostly they lost every time
Life meeting death

So she learned Death was always there
Many wondered why she thought about it all
Life meeting death

Yet her dreams and ghosts keep her aware
Life is special its precious
Yet so is death in its finality
Life meeting death

She fought to live
Beyond wars beyond cancer beyond overindulgence
Yet she never forgets
That her path is not finished
Knowing she cannot run forever
Soon it will be her time
Life meeting death

THE ART OF MEDICINE

My art is medicine
My business is caring
Many start it
Many find its science
Forgetting it's about people

Only a few get its true art
Its more than just caring
Its more than doing
It's being in the patient's moment
Carl Rodgers called it centered

Some get it
Some never will
They try
They fail
They just do the job
Never being an active participate
Service not advocacy
Forgetting it's not for them
But it's always been an art – people care

I CARED

For 45 years of life, I cared for others
Trauma ICU Disasters Hospice Long Term Care
Patients all needing hope and understanding and a sense of meaning
Forty years goes by, and I am now the case study I once studied and even taught

Age brings us change
Cardiac events thyroid storms,
Then the big C we all fear for living
Needing a place of Caring
Then I came to the Caring House
Where I found myself wondering about the if of tomorrows
Yet not alone among those with the same thoughts the same pain
All strangers then soon chosen family
Eating sleeping waiting for our treatment
Always in a place called Caring

At first there is this newness getting settled
Being aware of the reality of the situation
Avoiding self and avoiding others
Slowly meeting brothers and sisters in pain
Waiting
For the treatments
Good bad and at times ugly
Always returning to a place of Caring

We are all the same yet different
Same thoughts worries crying with fear of what is next
Soon I listen to others at lunch
Soon I reach out to others in the communal kitchen
Always in a place of Caring

Days of hurt and pain
Yet I return to a place greeted by a smile and concern
Always there to help me thru another day
Nurses doctors community members bringing food
Sharing our meals and talking with us
Just as people reaching out to people
Understanding listening holding our hands
Always in a place of Caring

This community of strangers becomes a chosen family
Together in worry yet separate in life
Living together in a place
The Caring House
Everyday someone says
I Care

EMT, RN, PA, PHD - ON SHE GOES

Fifty years goes fast

Learning how to practice medicine

Learning how to care for people

Learning what and how to separate diseases from complaints

Learning that the joy of medicine comes in little dosages

Learning how to separate the zebras from those running horses

Learning how to do the right things at the right time not just by protocol

Learning about people and their problems sometimes physical sometimes not

Learning how to be someone larger that oneself

Her fifty years went fast

Please can she have more

ACKNOWLEDGEMENTS:

- Please note: These poems are all works of fiction. These characters are so much more than what is written, and the words should never be confused with the living or the dead.

- All photographs in this volume are offered by the author

Life and Death
Skullspiration, Dia De Los Muertos street mural, listed by Gamma Galley taken in Denver, Colorado taken by KR Harbert in May 2018

The Tao Road To Taos
Harbert, KR, Published in Physician Assistant Education, Winter/ Spring 2002.

Enablers
Harbert, KR, Published in Perspectives on Physician Assistant Education, December 2002.

Harbert, KR, Life, Love and The Meditation Stone, Lulu, 2007.
An Eighty-Year-Old Man, Life, Love, and the Meditation Stone, Defining Life And Love Within A Sushi Bar, Home, Age, He Keeps On Trying, His Last Breath, Shadow Walk, Green Chile Cheeseburgers.

Why Do You Do What You Do
Harbert, KR, Published in Physician Assistant Education, Winter/ Spring 2002.

Memorial Day

Harbert, KR, Published in Military Writers Society of America, "Those Fought in Any Case: A Collection of Poems and Short Stories by Veterans", Summer 2022.

Life Savers then.... Caregivers Forever

Harbert, KR, Published in Military Writers Society of America, "Those Fought in Any Case: A Collection of Poems and Short Stories by Veterans", Summer 2022.

Will You Remember My Name

Harbert, KR, Published in TCFFFV Poetry Journal, Vol. 2, July 31, 2021.

The Hem/Onc Trip

Harbert, KR, Published in Journal of Physician Assistant Education, Vol. 18, 2007.

Echoes of the Future

Street mural by K. Zuckerman, K. Sweeney, R. Popowcer, M. Lutz in Albuquerque taken by KR Harbert on August, 20, 2005

God Loves The Grunts

print by George Skypect Jr. taken by KR Harbert

HEARTFELT APPRECIATION TO:

My first poetry readers Peggeen, Wanda, Benn, Renee, and Dedra.

Special thanks to Patrick Bizzaro and Shelly Benoit for letting my volume gain true meaning.

To Redhawk Publications' Robert Canipe, and especially Patty Thompson, for believing in this dream of mine.

To all those who have been there for me through big mistakes and small successes – bless you for believing in me no matter what.

ABOUT THE AUTHOR

Life to Ken is the appreciation of what makes us human, critical thinkers, always looking inward for understanding and meaning. After spending his life in clinical and academic medicine he is trying to be a good sailor, writer, poet, husband, father, grandfather. He keeps planning on doing more. His kids keep laughing.

www.ingramcontent.com/pod-product-compliance
Lightning Source LLC
Chambersburg PA
CBHW071641090426
42738CB00034B/2946